THE LITTLE BOOK OF
Book of Mormon Evidences

John Hilton III

DESERET
BOOK

Salt Lake City, Utah

Library of Congress Cataloging-in-Publication Data

Hilton, John, III.
 The little book of Book of Mormon evidences / John Hilton III.
     p. cm.
  Includes bibliographical references and index.
  ISBN 978-1-59038-850-1 (pbk.)
  1. Book of Mormon—Criticism, interpretation, etc. I. Title.
BX8627.H25 2007
289.3'22—dc22   2007042801

Printed in the United States of America
R. R. Donnelley and Sons, Crawfordsville, IN

10   9   8   7   6   5   4   3   2   1

To Opa John
a true scholar of the Book of Mormon

Contents

Acknowledgments

I am grateful to all those who contributed their time and talents to publishing this book. Particularly, I thank the many researchers who have uncovered the evidences that are presented herein. A portion of the proceeds from the sale of this book will go to fund further research.

A special thank-you to Noel Reynolds and Anthony Sweat, who showed me the value of teaching these evidences and provided ideas on how to do it.

Introduction

*Rational argument does not
create belief, but it maintains a climate
in which belief may flourish.*

Austin Farrer, on C. S. Lewis

When Elder Russell M. Nelson was working as a doctor, he once gave a copy of the Book of Mormon to a couple he worked with:

About a week later, they returned the book to him, saying, "Thanks a lot."

Rather assertively, Russell asked, "What do you mean, 'thanks a lot'? That is a totally inappropriate response for one who has read this book. You didn't read the book. Please take it back and read it; and then when you have read it, please return it to me."

Somewhat red-faced and embarrassed by this challenge and confrontation, the [couple] retrieved the book, acknowledging that they had only thumbed through the pages. Three weeks later, they returned with tears in their eyes and said, "We have read the book. We know it's true. We want to learn more." Dr. Nelson said, "Now I know you've read the book."

In due course, Dr. Nelson baptized the grateful couple.[1]

The Book of Mormon is an amazing book! Once I took my son Levi (then five years old) to a missionary fireside. At the end of the fireside, when they offered copies of the Book of Mormon, Levi took one and said he was excited to share it with a friend.

A couple of weeks later, Levi's friend Michael came to our house. Levi ran and got the Book of Mormon and gave it to him. "Here you go," Levi said. "It's a Book of Mormon."

"Thanks," Michael replied.

Levi looked at Michael, and Michael looked at him.

"Well," Levi said somewhat impatiently, "you can read it right now." Obediently, Michael opened the book and began reading.

I too love the Book of Mormon and know that it is the word of God. It was written by ancient prophets on the American continent and teaches of Jesus Christ and his gospel. President Ezra Taft Benson explained that the Book of Mormon is the "keystone of testimony."[2]

A keystone is the center stone in an arch. It literally holds the stones of the arch in place

Because the Book of Mormon is the "keystone of testimony," gaining a testimony of the Book of Mormon can be essential to obtaining a testimony of the Restoration. That's because (1) if the Book of Mormon is true, then you know Heavenly Father lives and Jesus Christ is our Savior. You also know Joseph Smith was a prophet. So (2) if Joseph Smith was a prophet, then you know that the Church he restored is true. Therefore, (3) if the Church is true, then you know it is led by a living prophet whose teachings come from God. Having a testimony of the Book of Mormon holds everything else in place.

As you know, the way to get a testimony of the Book of Mormon is to read it sincerely and pray about it. The last prophet in the Book of Mormon promised:

> And when ye shall *receive* these things, I would exhort you that ye would *ask* God, the Eternal Father, in the name of Christ, if these things are not true; and if ye shall *ask* with a

sincere heart, with real intent, having faith in Christ, he will manifest the truth of it unto you, by the power of the Holy Ghost.

And by the power of the Holy Ghost ye may know the truth of all things. (Moroni 10:4–5; emphasis added)

One of the most important things you and I can do is to take Moroni up on his promise and learn through the Holy Ghost that the Book of Mormon is true. *Ultimately, the only Book of Mormon evidence that matters is the evidence provided by the Holy Ghost.* At the same time, there is a lot of scholarly evidence on the Book of Mormon that can be helpful to know. Let me explain why.

In the accompanying illustration you see a large structure made out of pipes that is connected to the building under construction. This is called scaffolding, a temporary framework that allows workers to more easily finish the building. Once the construction is complete, the scaffolding is taken down.

In some ways scholarly evidence of the truthfulness of the Book of Mormon is like scaffolding. It's not the real testimony, but it can support
us while we are in the process of building and
deepening our testimony by providing an atmos-
phere in which testimony can grow. Sometimes
we might be confronted with the claims of those
who argue that the Book of Mormon is not true.
Knowing a little bit about Book of Mormon
evidences can be helpful at such times.

Once when I was a missionary, my companion
and I were teaching a family. During the lesson,

a family member said many negative things about the Church. When we left the home that day, I still had a testimony, but I was a little bit shaken by what the person had said.

At such a time, I was grateful for a grandfather who had taught me about a variety of scholarly evidences that supported the truthfulness of the Book of Mormon. Don't get me wrong—I still had my spiritual testimony, but at that difficult time the intellectual knowledge I had was a help—a scaffolding if you will—that allowed me to examine my understanding of the Church and make my testimony even stronger.

In addition, you may have had acquaintances who attacked your beliefs and demanded "proof" that the Book of Mormon is true. When that happens, knowing about wordprints, chiasmus, Hebraisms, and other evidences can be useful.

You've probably seen an object lesson in which somebody takes a stick and then snaps it in half.

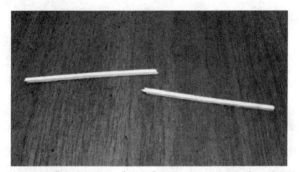

But when several sticks are put together in a bundle, they cannot be broken.

This object lesson can be likened to evidence that the Book of Mormon is true, with each piece of evidence being like a stick. In this little book you will read of statistical experiments, eleven witnesses, Hebraisms, and more than a dozen other pieces of evidence (sticks) that demonstrate that the Book of Mormon is exactly what it claims to be—ancient scripture. Individually, these scholarly pieces of evidence could be dismissed as "just a coincidence." None of them "proves" that the Book of Mormon is true, but taken together they provide a strong witness for its authenticity. And the more we know about them, the harder it will be for people to break our testimonies.

The truth is, the Book of Mormon *is* scripture. God *in reality* spoke to ancient prophets who lived on the American continent. And even though we do not need to "prove" it, I hope the evidences presented in this book reinforce your belief and help you share your testimony with others.

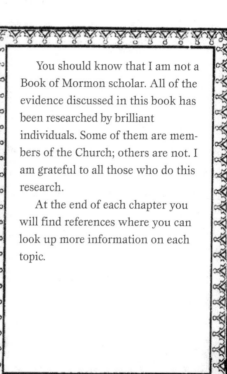

You should know that I am not a Book of Mormon scholar. All of the evidence discussed in this book has been researched by brilliant individuals. Some of them are members of the Church; others are not. I am grateful to all those who do this research.

At the end of each chapter you will find references where you can look up more information on each topic.

I

What's Up with Wordprints?

Have you ever heard of Theodore Kaczynski? Don't feel bad if you haven't, but his story is a fascinating one. More commonly known as the Unabomber, he planted sixteen bombs that injured twenty-nine individuals and killed three. Some of his bombs were planted in packages mailed to the victims. On one occasion he planted a bomb on an airplane. Fortunately, that bomb malfunctioned. Instead of exploding, it began emitting smoke, and all the passengers were able to get off the plane safely.

For sixteen years (from 1978 to 1995) the Unabomber was one of the most wanted criminals in the United States but managed to evade local and state police—even the FBI. So how did he finally get caught?

Well, the Unabomber had an agenda. He hated technology, and in 1995 the Unabomber demanded that a paper he had written about the dangers of technology be published in major newspapers. The *New York Times* and the *Washington Post* agreed to publish it, hoping that somebody would recognize his writing style. That's exactly what happened. On April 3, 1996, the Unabomber was arrested.

The Unabomber's brother tipped off the FBI, but before the brother contacted them, the FBI was working with a statistics professor at Brigham Young University. Now why would the FBI want a statistics professor's help in determining who wrote a manuscript? Because of wordprints.

Wordprints?

Yes, wordprints. They are like fingerprints. Let me explain.

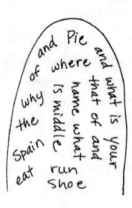

Just as people have unique fingerprints that identify them, writers have wordprints—writing patterns that are different and distinct from those of other writers. The way a writer uses simple words such as *the, a, of,* and others creates a pattern unique to that writer. Even when writers try to change the way they write, their wordprints follow them. And so the FBI wanted this BYU professor to compare the wordprints of several possible suspects to the wordprint of the Unabomber.

The professor the FBI contacted happened to

be John Hilton the first—my grandfather! I remember the excitement I felt when I learned that my grandfather's work was contributing to crime fighting. But that feeling was nothing compared to what I felt when I learned what his work with wordprints had to do with the Book of Mormon.

My grandfather first got into wordprints when he joined a group of scientists, several of whom were not Latter-day Saints, to do a test on the Book of Mormon. Because some people argued that Joseph Smith or Oliver Cowdery wrote it, the researchers wanted to compare their wordprints with those of the Book of Mormon. If their wordprints were different from the wordprints in the Book of Mormon, that difference would show that they did not write it.

Furthermore, as those who have read the Book of Mormon know, there are different authors throughout the book. The researchers decided to measure whether the wordprints of Alma and

Nephi were the same. If Alma and Nephi turned out to have different wordprints, that would establish that the Book of Mormon was written by more than one person.

I'll spare you the complicated details, but as you probably guessed, the researchers discovered that the Book of Mormon was *not* written by Joseph Smith or Oliver Cowdery. In fact, they discovered that it is "statistically indefensible to propose Joseph Smith or Oliver Cowdery" as the author of the Book of Mormon.[1]

My grandfather explained the researchers' results to me like this: Imagine everybody's wordprint measurements on a graph. Each person's wordprint occupies a specific location. If you have a document written by Oliver Cowdery, it would be clear that it was *his* writing and not somebody else's.

As the researchers studied the wordprints, it became obvious that each author was on a separate and distinct place on the graph.

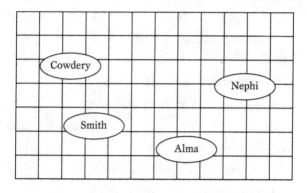

Simply stated, wordprints are legitimate measurements recognized not only by scholars but by the FBI. And wordprints statistically prove that Joseph Smith did not write the Book of Mormon—a great piece of evidence!

Additional Resources

G. Bruce Schaalje, John L. Hilton, and John B. Archer, "Comparative Power of Three Author-Attribution Techniques for Differentiating Authors," *Journal of Book of Mormon Studies* 6, no. 1 (1997): 47–65. Available at maxwellinstitute.byu.edu

John L. Hilton, "On Verifying Wordprint Studies: Book of Mormon Authorship," *BYU Studies* 30, no. 3 (1990): 89–108. Available at byustudies.byu.edu

What Would You Do If You Felt a Friend Betrayed You?

Lessons from Book of Mormon Witnesses

Consider the following hypothetical situation:

Lisa, Jennifer, and Susy had been friends for about a year. One day Lisa asked Jennifer if she would help her out. Lisa had a crush on Susy's boyfriend, Paul, and she wanted Jennifer to tell Susy a lie about Paul to get them to break up. Lisa promised Jennifer a hundred dollars if she would help her. Jennifer wasn't a bad person and didn't want to lie, but she needed money. So she told Susy a lie about Paul, and Susy broke up with him. Are you following all this?

But Lisa never paid Jennifer the hundred

Lisa
(told Jennifer
to lie)

Jennifer
(lied to
Susy)

Susy
(broke up
with Paul)

Paul

dollars. Even worse, Lisa started spreading lies about Jennifer throughout the school, and Jennifer was humiliated. One day Susy came up to Jennifer and said, "Listen, I know you lied to me about Paul in order to get us to break up, but that's okay. I forgive you. All I want is to get back at Lisa. Will you help me get back at her?"

If you were Jennifer, what would you do? I think Jennifer probably *would* help Susy because she was so angry with Lisa. This story can help us understand a little more about the witnesses of the Book of Mormon.

Three witnesses said they saw an angel of God

show them the plates. Eight other witnesses testified that they saw and held the plates, which were shown to them by Joseph Smith. If the testimony of these men is true, that is solid evidence of the authenticity of the Book of Mormon.

Now consider this. Of these eleven witnesses, many had serious arguments with Joseph Smith and left the Church. But *not one of them ever denied his testimony of the Book of Mormon.*

Think of it! If one of the witnesses had lied about seeing and holding the gold plates, he could have exposed Joseph Smith and the gold plates as a fraud! But nobody did. Let's learn a little more about the witnesses.

The Book of Mormon itself testified that some would be chosen as witnesses. Nephi recorded:

> Wherefore, at that day when the book shall be delivered unto the man of whom I have spoken, the book shall be hid from the eyes of the world, that the eyes of none shall behold it save it be that three witnesses shall behold it, by the

power of God, besides him to whom the book shall be delivered; and they shall testify to the truth of the book and the things therein.

And there is none other which shall view it, save it be a few according to the will of God, to bear testimony of his word unto the children of men. (2 Nephi 27:12–13)

Nephi taught that three individuals would see the plates by the power of God while a "few" (which can mean eight; see 1 Peter 3:20) would see the plates by the "will of God." The main difference between the Three and the Eight Witnesses is that the angel Moroni showed the plates to the Three Witnesses; Joseph Smith showed them to the Eight Witnesses.

Who exactly were these witnesses? Let's take a look.

The Three Witnesses

Oliver Cowdery. Oliver taught school and was a scribe to Joseph Smith in translating the Book of Mormon, but he later left the Church and became a lawyer. On one occasion, while in court, an opposing lawyer ridiculed Oliver Cowdery as a man who had claimed to have seen an angel and golden plates. By that time Oliver had not been involved with the Church for several years. It would have been easy to deny what he had seen, but instead he replied that his testimony "was literally true."[1] A couple of years before he died, Oliver rejoined the Church.

Martin Harris. A prominent farmer in Palmyra, New York, Martin provided Joseph Smith with money during the translation of the Book of Mormon. He was widely respected in the community and was elected by his community to positions of trust on many occasions. He also sacrificed part of his farm so the Book of Mormon could be published—something he would have never done if he did not truly believe! Martin also left the Church for a time, but eventually he rejoined and moved to Utah to live with the Saints.

David Whitmer. Like the other two of the Three Witnesses, David also left the Church; unlike them, however, he never came back. But though he lived to be more than eighty years old, he never denied his testimony. David was a respected citizen in his community, and for a time he served as mayor. At his death, one of the newspapers of his town said David Whitmer was "one of our oldest and best-known citizens."[2] Does that seem like the kind of person who would lie about his witness of the Book of Mormon?

On one occasion David was talking with a military officer who said that David had probably been deceived somehow by Joseph Smith. David stood up and said, "No sir! I was not under any hallucination, nor was I deceived! I saw with these eyes, and I heard with these ears! *I know whereof I speak!*"[3]

Just before he died, David published a letter in the newspaper testifying that he had in fact seen an angel and held the plates. More than fifty years after the Book of Mormon was published, he wrote, "I have never at any time denied [my] testimony. . . . Those who know me best, well know that I have always adhered to that testimony."[4]

The Eight Witnesses

Christian Whitmer. Although he was persecuted, and threatened with death by a mob, he never left the Church and never denied his testimony.

Peter Whitmer Jr. Like his brother Christian, Peter never denied his testimony nor left the faith.

Hiram Page. Hiram was one of the first converts to the Church and held a variety of leadership positions. During the struggles in Missouri, he grew bitter against the Church and no longer associated with it. Though he did not return to the Church, he never denied his testimony of the Book of Mormon.

Jacob Whitmer. Like Hiram Page, Jacob left the Church after persecutions in Missouri. Decades later, his only surviving son said, "My father (Jacob Whitmer) was always faithful and true to his testimony in regard to the Book of Mormon, and confirmed it on his deathbed."[5]

Joseph Smith Sr. The Prophet's father, Joseph Smith Senior, never wavered in his witness of the Book of Mormon or his testimony of the Church.

Hyrum Smith. Hyrum, like his brother Joseph, sealed his witness of the Book of Mormon with his blood (D&C 135:3).

John Whitmer. John held many important positions in the Church, including that of Church Historian. Later, however, he was excommunicated from the Church and became extremely bitter toward Joseph Smith. Still, on one occasion in the presence of several Missourians who hated the Church, he testified of the Book of Mormon and witnessed that he had handled the plates.

Samuel H. Smith. The Prophet's younger brother Samuel remained true to the Church and never denied his testimony.

Think of it! Eleven different men, six of whom left the Church, yet none ever denied his testimony of the Book of Mormon. These were honest and upstanding men in the community. If they had been making up the whole thing, don't you think at least one of the witnesses would have changed his story?

But none of them ever did. And that provides eleven sticks of powerful evidence that their witness is true.

Additional Resource

Richard Lloyd Anderson, *Book of Mormon Witnesses.* Available at maxwellinstitute.byu.edu

How Fast Can You Write a Research Paper?
The Translation of the Book of Mormon

Have you ever had to write a research paper? When I was in college, I often received assignments to write a paper at the end of a semester. I thought this was a huge challenge. I would have to go to the library, check out books, find resources, edit, revise, rewrite—it was hard! As I compare my experience writing research papers with the conditions under which Joseph Smith worked, I realize just how amazing the translation of the Book of Mormon was.

Consider the following fact:

Joseph Smith had very little formal education. His wife Emma said that Joseph "could neither write nor dictate a coherent and well-worded letter."[1] If Joseph struggled with basic writing, it seems very unlikely he could have written the Book of Mormon on his own. Observers of the translation process also said that Joseph Smith used no notes or anything of the kind. So he couldn't have been reading from another source while he translated.

Something else that amazes me about the translation process is that when Joseph and his scribe returned from having taken a break for meals or resting, Joseph always picked up *exactly* where they had left off—without looking at the manuscript or asking to have some of it read back to him.

Think about things you have written. Could you do that? As I wrote this book, I frequently had to look back to see what I had already written and where I had left off before beginning a new day of writing.

To use Emma's words about her husband, "It

would have been improbable that a learned man could [begin translating again without looking to see where he had been]; and, for one so ignorant and unlearned as he was, it was simply impossible."[2]

Impossible, that is, unless Joseph was truly inspired in translating the plates—which he was!

Getting back to research papers: how long does it take you to write them? You're probably faster than I was, but it usually took several hours to write just a couple of quality pages. If you had a paper due tomorrow, how many pages do you think you could write in the next twenty-four hours? What quality of text would you be able to produce on such short notice?

Thinking about these questions helps me realize how amazing the Book of Mormon is. Joseph Smith translated most of the Book of Mormon in less than three months—and that wasn't the only thing he was doing. During this time, he also received the Aaronic and Melchizedek

Priesthoods, received thirteen revelations that are now in the Doctrine and Covenants, and worked to support his family. While doing all of that, Joseph Smith translated the Book of Mormon at a rate of about eight pages per day!

At that pace, it would have taken Joseph Smith a day and a half to write King Benjamin's farewell address (Mosiah 2–5). Do you think you could write such a discourse that fast? I know I couldn't.

As a college professor, before being called to the Quorum of the Twelve Apostles, Elder David A. Bednar wrote a book. He shared how writing this book deepened his understanding of how Joseph Smith could *not* have written the Book of Mormon:

> One of the books I authored with a colleague . . . is 650 pages long, it contains 17 chapters, and it took us two years to write. The colleague with whom I wrote this book also has a Ph.D., which means that we each went to college for

eight years or more—a total of more than 16 years of formal higher education between the two of us. It is a remarkable experience to receive a box of these brand-new books from the publisher. . . . I opened up the box and thumbed through one of the books. As I did so, I looked out the window of my office and asked myself the question, "Why did you write this book?" When you really think about it, investing so much time and effort in a project that so quickly becomes obsolete is rather foolish. As I posed that question to myself and as I was pondering, the thought came to me, "Because now you know by experience that Joseph Smith could not have written the Book of Mormon." . . .

With eight years of university training, with two years of very dedicated work, with an editorial staff, with personal computers, with spell checkers and thesauruses on-line, with the Internet and the other resources that are so readily available, when I picked up the book that I had written and opened it up, I still found mistakes. And within a matter of twelve months, this book upon which I had worked so hard and so long was obsolete and had to be revised. . . .

I know as an author and by personal experience that Joseph Smith could not and did not write the Book of Mormon.[3]

That quotation from Elder Bednar says it all. Considering Joseph Smith's lack of education and the conditions under which he translated the Book of Mormon, there is no way he could have just made it up, as some people claim. Just as with Elder Bednar's book, our own experience with writing should help to make clear in our minds that the Book of Mormon is the work of God, not the work of man.

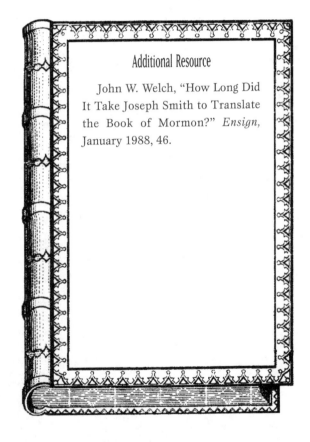

Additional Resource

John W. Welch, "How Long Did It Take Joseph Smith to Translate the Book of Mormon?" *Ensign,* January 1988, 46.

4

"Handsome Boy!"
Hebrew in the Book of Mormon

When I visited China for the first time, I went to a place called Seven Star Crags. It is a beautiful place, and though there were many Chinese tourists, there were very few Americans. I was enjoying the scenery with my brother Cameron and our friends Shao Wenhui, Zhang Lin, and Wu Cuiling, when a Chinese woman approached me and said, "Handsome boy, may I have my picture taken with you?"

I was flattered! It isn't every day that somebody calls me "handsome boy!" Later, one of our Chinese friends told us that in that area of China, the polite way to refer to a male stranger is *shuài ge* ("handsome boy")—kind of like saying "sir" in English. So even though it sounded flattering in English, it wasn't meant to be that way in Chinese. This kind of confusion can happen when you translate from one language to another.

That happened once when, as my family and I were kneeling down to pray, I said to one of my children, "Would you please make a prayer for us?" I know that sounds strange—normally one would ask, "Would you please say the prayer?"

But at the time, I was speaking Spanish frequently, and in Spanish when you invite somebody to say a prayer, you say, "Quiere hacer la oracion?" (literally, "Will you make the prayer?"). Because I frequently invited people to pray in Spanish, when I asked somebody to pray in English, my request came out with English words in a Spanish form.

If you frequently interact with people who speak languages different from your own, you may have noticed similar examples when they use the structure of another language in expressing themselves.

Interestingly, this same effect is found in the Book of Mormon because the authors were familiar with the Hebrew way of thinking and writing. In the second verse of his record Nephi writes, "Yea, I make a record in the language of my father, which consists of the *learning of the Jews*" (1 Nephi 1:2, emphasis added). If the Book of Mormon was really written by Nephi and other prophets familiar with Hebrew, we would expect the Hebrew form of thinking to frequently appear in their writing.

And it does! The term scholars use when a Hebrew form of thinking or writing shows up in English is *Hebraism,* and the Book of Mormon is full of Hebraisms.

As I learned about the following examples, I said to myself, "There is no way Joseph Smith, even if he knew Hebrew (which he didn't at the time he was translating the Book of Mormon) could have inserted so many Hebraisms into the book—either on purpose or by accident. The only logical explanation is that he was translating a book written by people who spoke and thought in Hebrew or a similar language." Let's check it out.

"A Plastic Doll" or "A Doll of Plastic"?

Suppose you bought your little sister a plastic doll. Would you say, "I bought you a plastic doll" or "I bought you a doll of plastic"? Obviously, in English we would say "a plastic doll." In Hebrew, however, when a noun is used to describe another noun, frequently the word *of* is used to connect them. Therefore, in the Hebrew language you would say "doll of plastic."

This Hebraism is found throughout the Book of Mormon—and you're familiar with many of these references. Although we say "brass plates," the phrase does not appear in the Book of Mormon. On the other hand, the phrase "plates of brass" appears twenty-seven times. We sing about "the iron rod," but Nephi never wrote about it. The phrase "rod of iron," however, is recorded eight times. We never read about "Laban's sword" but always "the sword of Laban."

"My friends and I are going to a party" or "I and my friends are going to a party"

Even if you don't get good grades in English class, you should know that to say "I and my friends . . ." is not considered good grammar. Didn't our mothers teach us to put others first? The proper thing to say is "My friends and I . . ." In Hebrew, however, the correct way to write about you and your friends is "I and my friends."

Interesting, isn't it? A phrase that is poor English is actually good Hebrew! And in nearly every instance in the Book of Mormon, the writer puts the *I* first. For example, consider the following verses:

"Behold, I and my brethren will go forth into the land of Zarahemla" (Alma 27:15).

"Thus far I and my father had kept the

commandments wherewith the Lord had commanded us" (1 Nephi 5:20).

"I and my people did cry mightily to the Lord" (Mosiah 9:17).

Dreaming Dreams

"Behold," Lehi says, "I have dreamed a dream" (1 Nephi 8:2).

"Well, of course!" you might say. "What else would you dream?"

The phrase "I have dreamed a dream" is certainly not common in English. But in Hebrew that is exactly the phrase you would use if you wanted to emphasize the importance of your dream—as Lehi certainly did before telling his children about his vision of the tree of life.

"Cite Your Minds Forward"

In Alma 13:1, Alma says, "I would cite your minds forward to the time when the Lord God gave these commandments unto his children."

In English, if somebody said we were going *forward* in time, we would think about the future. But after saying, "I would cite your minds forward," Alma begins to talk about the *past*—the premortal life. That does not make sense—at least not in English! In fact, some have said that this verse proves the Book of Mormon is not true, for how can you "cite" someone's mind "forward" to something that happened in the past?

Interestingly enough, in Hebrew things that are in the future are spoken of as being "behind" and things in the past "ahead." In the Hebrew way of thinking, "cite your minds forward" would mean to go toward the beginning. So this phrase is evidence not that the Book of Mormon is false but that it was written by those familiar with the Hebrew way of expression.

How Old Are You?

"I am twenty and nine years old." That doesn't sound quite right, does it? In modern English we would say "twenty-nine"—the *and* is not needed. But as you've probably guessed, in Hebrew an *and* is used to connect compound numbers between twenty-one and ninety-nine. All numbers in the Book of Mormon use this Hebraic format. Consider, for example, the following examples:

"After that ye are seventy and two years old ye shall . . ." (3 Nephi 28:3).

"And in the fifty and first year of the reign of the judges there was peace" (Helaman 3:33).

"And it came to pass that two hundred and thirty and eight years had passed away" (Jarom 1:13).

These are just five of many Hebraisms used throughout the Book of Mormon. Just as somebody would not say in English, "Do you want to make the last prayer," unless they were thinking in Spanish, these Hebraisms would not have appeared if the authors of the Book of Mormon had not been thinking in Hebrew. Of course, Hebraisms do not prove that the Book of Mormon is true, but they do provide more "sticks" to show that the Book of Mormon is exactly what it claims to be.

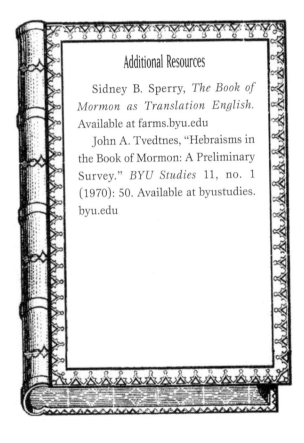

Additional Resources

Sidney B. Sperry, *The Book of Mormon as Translation English.* Available at farms.byu.edu

John A. Tvedtnes, "Hebraisms in the Book of Mormon: A Preliminary Survey." *BYU Studies* 11, no. 1 (1970): 50. Available at byustudies. byu.edu

5

Poetry in the Book of Mormon?

When I think about poetry, I usually think of phrases that rhyme.

But poems don't have to rhyme
All of the time.

Only some kinds of poetry rhyme. In fact, different forms of poetry have different requirements. For example, haiku requires a certain number of syllables in each line. Before I explain more, answer these two questions:

Did you learn about haiku in school?

If yes, do you remember what the formula is for haiku?

If you answered yes to the second question,

you are a better student than I was! I had to look up *haiku* to relearn the pattern, which is a seventeen-syllable poem, typically written in lines of five, seven, and five syllables, like this:

> *Tom and Jill went out.*
> *It was their very first date.*
> *They had a great time.*

Okay, so my poetry skills aren't great, but hopefully this helps you understand what a haiku is. The point I am trying to make is this: even though I learned about haiku in school, I have *never,* until now, written a haiku in any book or paper. Haiku is not something that you write accidentally. I'll explain why that's important in just a moment.

Another form of poetry is called chiasmus. A chiasmus is perhaps even more difficult to write than haiku. It is based on a series of phrases or themes leading up to a central point and then touching on each of the topics or themes in reverse. Like this:

Phrase A
  Phrase B
    Phrase C
      Phrase D
        Main Point
        Main Point[1] [Sometimes the main point in the center is not repeated.]
      Phrase D'
    Phrase C'
  Phrase B'
Phrase A'

As you can see, there is a parallel symmetry in the chiasmus. Here is another example:

(a) Once I was feeling bored.
  (b) I turned on the television,
    (c) But what I saw was not good.
      (d) So I opened my scriptures.
        (e) As I read the scriptures I felt the Spirit.
        (e') A Spirit of peace descended on me as I read.
      (d') My open scriptures guided me.
    (c') They led me to that which was good.
  (b') I threw away my television.
(a') Now I am no longer bored.

About this time you may be thinking, *This is nice, but what does poetry have to do with the Book of Mormon?* I'll sum it up in three points and then explain:

Chiasmus is a significant form of poetry used by the Hebrews.

Chiasmus is also a form of poetry found in the Book of Mormon.

Because Joseph Smith did not know about chiasmus when he translated the Book of Mormon, chiasmus provides remarkable evidence that the Book of Mormon was in fact written by people familiar with the Hebrew language (like the Nephites).

Chiasmus Is a Form of Poetry Used by the Hebrews

We have many examples of chiasmus written by ancient Hebrews. For example, in Genesis 7:21–23 we read the following chiasmus:

(a) And all flesh died that moved upon the earth,

  (b) both of fowl,

    (c) and of cattle, and of beast, and of every creeping thing that creepeth upon the earth,

      (d) and every man:

        (e) All in whose nostrils was the breath of life, of all that was in the dry land, died.

        (e') And every living substance was destroyed which was upon the face of the ground,

      (d') both man,

    (c') and cattle, and the creeping things,

  (b') and the fowl of the heaven;

(a') and they were destroyed from the earth: and Noah only remained alive, and they that were with him in the ark.

Chiasmus is found frequently in the Bible, and it is evident that it is an intentional form of poetry—not something that was written just by accident.

Chiasmus Is Also a Form of Poetry Found in the Book of Mormon

Dozens of examples of chiasmus have been found in the Book of Mormon. In some cases (like Alma 36), a whole chapter is a giant chiasmus. Consider the following example from Mosiah 5:10–12 (emphasis added):

(a) And now it shall come to pass, that whosoever shall not take upon him the NAME of Christ

  (b) must be CALLED by some other name;

    (c) therefore, he findeth himself on the LEFT HAND of God.

      (d) And I would that ye should REMEMBER also, that this is the NAME

        (e) that I said I should give unto you that never should be BLOTTED OUT,

          (f) except it be through TRANSGRESSION;

          (f') therefore, take heed that ye do not TRANSGRESS,

        (e') that the name be not BLOTTED OUT of your hearts.

      (d') I say unto you, I would that ye should REMEMBER to retain the NAME

    (c') written always in your hearts, that ye are not found on the LEFT HAND of God,

  (b') but that ye hear and know the voice by which ye shall be CALLED,

(a') and also, the NAME by which he shall call you.

Joseph Smith knew nothing about chiasmus when he translated the Book of Mormon, so he could not have intentionally inserted it into the book. In fact, in the 1820s few scholars were even aware of chiasmus in the Bible! And just as I've never "accidentally" written haiku, it is *extremely* unlikely that the type of chiasmus found in the Book of Mormon happened by accident. So, because chiasmus is a form of ancient poetry and it also appears in the Book of Mormon, what does this tell us?

Simply stated, it tells us that the Book of Mormon is an ancient record, written by people who knew and understood this form of poetry.

Many chiasmus scholars who are *not* members of the Church have stated that the appearance of chiasmus in the Book of Mormon is something they have no explanation for. In fact, the only satisfying explanation for chiasmus in the Book of Mormon is the one Joseph Smith gave—that he in fact translated an ancient record written by prophets who came from the land of Jerusalem.

Now, don't base your testimony on chiasmus. The way to gain a testimony of the Book of

Mormon is to follow the counsel given in Moroni 10:4–5. But chiasmus does provide an interesting piece of evidence you can show your friends, right in the words of the book itself.

> *Congratulations!*
> *You have finished this chapter.*
> *Now you are smarter.*

(That was a haiku!)

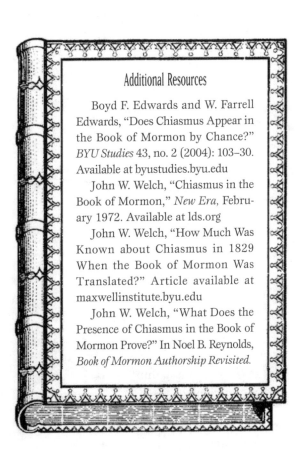

Additional Resources

Boyd F. Edwards and W. Farrell Edwards, "Does Chiasmus Appear in the Book of Mormon by Chance?" *BYU Studies* 43, no. 2 (2004): 103–30. Available at byustudies.byu.edu

John W. Welch, "Chiasmus in the Book of Mormon," *New Era*, February 1972. Available at lds.org

John W. Welch, "How Much Was Known about Chiasmus in 1829 When the Book of Mormon Was Translated?" Article available at maxwellinstitute.byu.edu

John W. Welch, "What Does the Presence of Chiasmus in the Book of Mormon Prove?" In Noel B. Reynolds, *Book of Mormon Authorship Revisited.*

6

"Gotcha Now"–or So They Thought

People have been criticizing the Book of Mormon for more than a century. In fact, the first articles criticizing the Book of Mormon appeared before it was even published! It is interesting to look at criticisms people made of the Book of Mormon in the past and see how modern research has shown that those criticisms are not valid.

For example, in 1929, Heber J. Grant, who was then president of the Church, recalled:

When I was a young unmarried man, another young man who had received a doctor's degree ridiculed me for believing in the Book of Mormon. [He said that one lie in the Book of

Mormon] was that the people had built their homes out of cement and that they were very skilful in the use of cement. He said there had never been found and never would be found, a house built of cement by the ancient inhabitants of this country, because the people in that early age knew nothing about cement. He said that should be enough to make one disbelieve the book. I said: "That does not affect my faith one particle. I read the Book of Mormon prayerfully and supplicated God for a testimony in my heart and soul of the divinity of it, and I have accepted it and believe it with all my heart." I also said to him, "If my children do not find cement houses, I expect that my grandchildren will." . . . Now, since that time houses made of cement and massive structures of the same material have been uncovered.[1]

Think of it! When President Grant was a young man, there was absolutely *no* evidence that the people in ancient America used cement, yet the Book of Mormon talks about the people using cement (see Helaman 3:7). You can see how some people would use this as a justification for critical comments.

Yet, in 1929, when he was a grandfather, President Grant was able to tell about remarkable discoveries of ancient cement houses. Scholars have continued to find cement used in ancient America. So President Grant was right. Do you remember what he said? "If my children do not find cement houses, I expect that my grandchildren will."

Evidence has since been found that contradicts a claim that people once said proved the Book of Mormon false. How could Joseph Smith have known there was cement in ancient America? Now that's *solid evidence* that the Book of Mormon is true. (Get it? "Solid," like concrete. Okay, that was a bad pun. . . . Let's keep going.)

There are many other instances in which anti-Mormon writers have said, "The Book of Mormon can't be true because . . . ," but evidence later turns up to prove their arguments false. Let's take a look at a few examples.

Alma

Two people in the Book of Mormon are named Alma. When I was in high school, the only time I heard the name *Alma* was when people were talking about the Book of Mormon. But when I went on my mission, I met a woman named Alma. I thought it was kind of funny—a woman named Alma! But then I learned that *Alma* is a common female name in Spanish. In fact some of the people I taught might have thought it was funny that in the Book of Mormon *Alma* is a man's name.

Critics of the Book of Mormon, trying to prove that the Book of Mormon isn't true, accused Joseph Smith of using the name *Alma* in the Book of Mormon without realizing it was a woman's name. Then, in the 1960s, a Jewish (*not* LDS) scholar found a document that dated back to the time of Lehi. One of the names on this document was (you guessed it)—Alma, the *son* of Judah. So Alma was an ancient male Hebrew name after all! There's no way Joseph Smith could have known that!

The Land Bountiful

Nephi wrote that when his family was traveling in the wilderness, they found a place that had fruit, was close to mountains, had enough wood and metal resources that they could build a ship, and also had a launching point so they could get their ship into the sea (see 1 Nephi 17:6–7, 16; 18:8).

"Yeah, right," some critics have said. "Where are you going to find all of that in the deserts of Arabia? It doesn't exist!"

And yet there *is* a place on the Arabian Peninsula that meets these characteristics. Nephi told us that his family left Jerusalem and went to the borders of the Red Sea. Then they traveled southeast for a few days and then east for a long time. Amazingly enough, if you follow this same route, you arrive at a location known today as Wadi Sayq. This spot (as well as some others) closely matches Nephi's description of Bountiful.

Think for a moment of how amazing that is. Even twenty years ago people did not believe that such a place existed and criticized the Book of Mormon. But now we can see that the place did (and does) exist.

Another stick!

Barley

Barley is a grain similar to wheat that has been grown in the Middle East for centuries. It is also found in America; however, in the 1800s scholars believed that barley was brought to America by the Europeans and that it *did not* exist in America before Columbus.

As you can imagine, some people made fun of the Book of Mormon for mentioning barley. "It can't be true," they said. But in 1983 a science magazine reported a discovery of barley on the American continent—barley that was dated to before the time of Christopher Columbus. So barley was in America before the Europeans came! I guess that's another instance of a Book of Mormon critic having to eat his words. (Get it? "Eating" in a section on barley? Okay, that was not funny. There's something about this chapter that makes me want to make bad puns. We'd better make this next example the last one.)

Elephants

In all of the standard works, elephants are mentioned in just one verse: Ether 9:19. Speaking of the Jaredites, it says, "And they also had horses, and asses, and there were elephants and cureloms and cumoms; all of which were useful unto man, and more especially the elephants and cureloms and cumoms."

As you already know, elephants are found in

Africa and Asia but *not* in America. So once again, critics said, "The Book of Mormon can't be true."

But (once again), scholarly research now points to evidence that elephants, or close relatives of them, *did* live in America at approximately the same time as the Jaredites.

This is a picture of fossil remains found on the American continent. Would you say that it looks like an elephant?

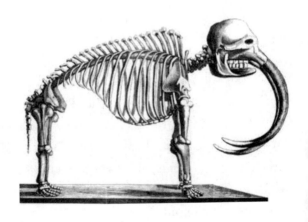

"And thus we see" that something once used to demonstrate that the Book of Mormon was false now proves to be evidence that the Book of Mormon is *true.*

Cement, Alma, Bountiful, barley, and elephants—five examples of things once used to ridicule the Book of Mormon that have been validated by modern scholars. This is a key point, because in the future someone may make a claim that says, "The Book of Mormon cannot be true because of such and such a thing."

Just because the Book of Mormon mentions something that appears not to be possible (such as elephants) does not prove that the Book of Mormon is false. Like President Heber J. Grant, if we are confronted with something we do not have an answer for, let us say, "If my children do not find an answer to that question, I expect that my grandchildren will!"

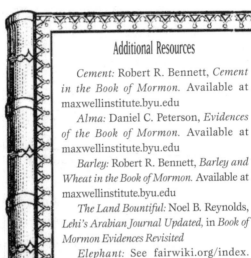

Additional Resources

Cement: Robert R. Bennett, *Cement in the Book of Mormon.* Available at maxwellinstitute.byu.edu

Alma: Daniel C. Peterson, *Evidences of the Book of Mormon.* Available at maxwellinstitute.byu.edu

Barley: Robert R. Bennett, *Barley and Wheat in the Book of Mormon.* Available at maxwellinstitute.byu.edu

The Land Bountiful: Noel B. Reynolds, *Lehi's Arabian Journal Updated,* in *Book of Mormon Evidences Revisited*

Elephant: See fairwiki.org/index.php/Book_of_Mormon_anachronisms: Animals

Other evidences once used to criticize the Book of Mormon: See fairwiki.org/index.php/FAIRwiki:Table_of_contents#Anachronisms.3F

7

Seven More Sticks

We've talked about several evidences of the authenticity of the Book of Mormon. Now I'd like to share with you seven more sticks (to use our bundle of sticks analogy) that show that the Book of Mormon really is what it claims to be.

Books in a Treasury

Where do you keep your books? Depending on how much you like them, you might put them on a bookshelf or under your bed. But would you ever consider putting them in a treasury? I wouldn't, but in 1 Nephi 4:20 we read that Nephi "went forth unto the treasury of Laban," where the brass plates were kept. I would never have thought of keeping records in a treasury! But research has shown that anciently people did keep their books in treasuries.[1]

Nephi's Bow and Arrow: Right on Target

In 1 Nephi 16:18 we read, "And it came to pass that as I, Nephi, went forth to slay food, behold, I did break my bow, which was made of fine steel; and after I did break my bow, behold, my brethren were angry with me because of the loss of my bow, for we did obtain no food."

You know what happens next, right?

True or false: Nephi used his old arrows, along with a new bow that he made, to hunt some food for his family.

Though it's almost true, the previous statement is actually *false.* Let's look at 1 Nephi 16:23: "I, Nephi, did make out of wood a bow, and out of a straight stick, an arrow; wherefore, I did arm myself with a bow and an arrow."

Why did Nephi have to make an arrow? It was

only his bow that broke! To answer this question we just need to reread 1 Nephi 16:18. Remember, Nephi wrote, "My bow, *which was made of fine steel*" (emphasis added). Archery experts know that an arrow designed for a steel bow would not work well with a wooden bow. But it's very unlikely that Joseph Smith could have known that!

A "River of Water"

Elder Jeffrey R. Holland, then of the Quorum of the Seventy, shared a Book of Mormon evidence that touched his heart as a young man:

> I can still remember the scriptural awakening that came to me when a skillful and well-prepared seminary teacher, teaching that much-read and, to us students, absolutely boring material from Nephi. I can remember when he asked me, in class, why in 1 Nephi 2:6 the Book of Mormon records that Lehi "pitched his tent in a valley by the side of a river of water."

Well, it was early in the year, only the first day or two of class, and as always, the teacher was still very much on trial. Being the smart-aleck student I almost always was, I made some clever response about it being smarter to pitch a tent by the side of a river rather than in it. . . . I knew I was a hit because the girls giggled.

The teacher didn't giggle. He smiled and he said, with the smile still on his face, "You're not answering the question, Jeff, because you're not reading the text. It doesn't say that Lehi pitched his tent by the river or in the river; it says he pitched it by a river of water. Why did he say a river of water, Jeff? What other kinds of rivers are there, Jeff?"[2]

The young student didn't know what to say. What other kinds of rivers are there, anyway? His teacher went on to explain to the class that in the deserts of Arabia there are rivers of sand as well as rivers of water. Although you and I might have thought that the only kinds of rivers were rivers of water, Nephi knew different;

therefore, he specified what kind of river it was. This short phrase, "river of water," provides simple evidence that the Book of Mormon was written by somebody familiar with Arabic geography. Joseph Smith was not!

Nahom

While Lehi and his family journeyed across the Arabian desert, "it came to pass that Ishmael died, and was buried in the place which was called Nahom. And it came to pass that the daughters of Ishmael did mourn exceedingly, because of the loss of their father" (1 Nephi 16:34–35).

The word *Nahom* does not appear in the Bible, so critics of the Book of Mormon say that Joseph Smith made it up. If he did make it up, he was really lucky, because (1) a related word in Hebrew means "to mourn" (notice that's what the daughters of Ishmael did at the place called Nahom), and (2) archaeologists recently discovered a place in the Arabian desert named NHM. Because Hebrew does not use vowels, this word can be translated into English in several ways. One of those is Nahom.

Not only was the name right, but it was in the right geographic location. There's no way Joseph Smith could have made *that* up!

Incredible Quoting

In Alma 36, Alma the Younger tells his son Helaman about his conversion. In verse 22, Alma describes how wonderful that experience was by saying he thought he "saw, even as our father Lehi saw, *God sitting upon his throne, surrounded with numberless concourses of angels, in the attitude of singing and praising their God*; yea, and my soul did long to be there" (emphasis added).

That passage is found on page 299 in my copy of the Book of Mormon. Now notice how Alma is actually *quoting* from Lehi—back on page 2!

"[Lehi] saw *God sitting upon his throne, surrounded with numberless concourses of angels in the attitude of singing and praising their God*" (1 Nephi 1:8). Comparing 1 Nephi 1:8 and Alma 36:22, you can easily see that Alma was making a direct quotation.

Do you remember that witnesses to the translation process said Joseph Smith never had his scribes read the translation back to him? It is *extremely* unlikely that he could have quoted what happened to Lehi when translating from the book of Alma.

Like me, you have probably read the Book of Mormon many times and never noticed this quotation! Another stick . . .

Conjunction Junction—What's Your Function?

After my mission I took an advanced writing class. My professor was so appalled by my poor grammar that she lent me the *Schoolhouse Rock* series to review basic grammar principles. From this program I learned that a conjunction is a word used to connect words and phrases. For example, in the phrase "bread and butter" the word *and* is the conjunction.

But conjunctions are not the only way to connect words together. If you are writing about a list of things, you can connect them with commas, like this: "I like to eat fish, chips, lemonade, and cookies. It would obviously sound pretty weird if you said, "I like to eat fish AND chips AND lemonade AND cookies."

So what's up with Helaman 3:14? It says, "But behold, a hundredth part of the proceedings of this people, yea, the account of the Lamanites AND of the Nephites, AND their wars, AND contentions, AND dissensions, AND their preaching, AND their prophecies, AND their shipping AND their building of ships, AND their building of temples, AND of synagogues AND their sanctuaries, AND their righteousness, AND their wickedness, AND their murders, AND their robbings, AND their plundering, AND all manner of abominations AND whoredoms, cannot be contained in this work" (emphasis added).

Surely, even with little education, Joseph Smith should have known not to use all those *ands!* But in Hebrew a conjunction (like *and*) is used to connect all words because commas don't exist. So this verse is an example of not-so-good English but great Hebrew—something Joseph Smith could not have known.

The Olive Trees

You have probably noticed that the longest chapter in the Book of Mormon (Jacob 5) has an extensive discussion of olive trees. I have never seen an olive tree in person, and maybe you haven't either.

Here's what they look like:

Jacob 5 goes into great detail about olive trees. Consider the following details:

Wild and tame olive trees are grafted together to strengthen the roots (Jacob 5:10–11).

Pruning is an important part of caring for olive trees (Jacob 5:27).

Digging around olive trees helps them grow (Jacob 5:27).

Fertilizer (in this case dung, or manure) is important in caring for olive trees (Jacob 5:64).

Pruning an olive tree too rapidly can be harmful to the tree (Jacob 5:65).

Each of these details presented in the Book of Mormon reflects the proper care of olive trees. Many other details in Jacob 5 are also in harmony with what we know today about raising olive trees.

Joseph Smith had never seen an olive tree and did not know anything about growing them—yet once again, the Book of Mormon is correct.

Additional Resources

I used the following Internet resources in writing this chapter. You can find many more great evidences in these places as well.

fairwiki.org/index.php/Olive_culture_in_the_Book_of_Mormon

jefflindsay.com/BMEvidences.shtml

lightplanet.com/response/bofm.htm

Noel B. Reynolds, *The Authorship of the Book of Mormon.* Available at speeches.byu.edu

Daniel Peterson, *Evidences of the Book of Mormon.* Available at maxwellinstitute.byu.edu

Conclusion

Wordprints. Witnesses. Chiasmus. Hebraisms. We've talked about many pieces of evidence that clearly show that Joseph Smith *did not* write the Book of Mormon. This leads us to the question: If he didn't write it, who did?

The only logical answer is the one given by Joseph Smith himself: The book was written by ancient prophets living on the American continent. For me, the most important evidence that the Book of Mormon was written by prophets is the feeling I get from the Holy Ghost when I diligently study the book. You can have this same feeling.

After a fireside in which I talked about evidences from the Book of Mormon, I was approached by a young woman I'll call Elizabeth.

Elizabeth was a very intelligent young woman. She wanted to know how she could find out for certain that the Book of Mormon was true.

As I talked with her, I discovered that although she read several books each week, she had never read the Book of Mormon and she had never prayed about it. By the end of our conversation, she came up with a plan to find out whether the Book of Mormon was true.

She decided to read the Book of Mormon twenty minutes a day for a month. Before and after reading it each day, she would pray, asking for guidance from the Lord.

I haven't seen Elizabeth since that day, but I commend the same formula to you. The witness of the Spirit will be the most important "stick" of testimony you will receive that the Book of Mormon is true. As we continue to study the Book of Mormon and make it the keystone of our testimony, we will be on solid ground.

No matter what concern or doubt people have

about a teaching of the Church, it can be resolved if they know that the Book of Mormon is true. President Ezra Taft Benson put it this way:

All objections, whether they be on abortion, plural marriage, seventh-day worship, etc., basically hinge on whether Joseph Smith and his successors were and are prophets of God receiving divine revelation. Here, then, is a procedure to handle most objections through the use of the Book of Mormon.

First, understand the objection.

Second, give the answer from revelation.

Third, show how the correctness of the answer really depends on whether or not we have modern revelation through modern prophets.

Fourth, explain that whether or not we have modern prophets and revelation really depends on whether the Book of Mormon is true.

Therefore, the only problem the objector has to resolve for himself is whether the Book of Mormon is true. For if the Book of Mormon is true, then Jesus is the Christ, Joseph Smith was

His prophet, The Church of Jesus Christ of Latter-day Saints is true, and it is being led today by a prophet receiving revelation.[1]

This procedure works on an individual level for any number of situations. Suppose you are a teenage boy who wants to take his girlfriend on a date every week. But the pamphlet *For the Strength of Youth* says, "Avoid going on frequent dates with the same person" (27). You would simply need to ask yourself, "Is the Book of Mormon true or not?"

If it is, then you know the Church is true and is led by a living prophet today and you should follow the counsel he gives.

Let's take a look at how a missionary could use this "procedure" given by President Benson to help resolve an investigator's concern.

* * *

MISSIONARY: The Word of Wisdom is a law of health given by revelation. It says that we should not drink alcohol, coffee, or tea, and we should not smoke tobacco.

INVESTIGATOR: I don't drink alcohol or smoke, but I do drink tea—my doctor told me that it would be good for me.

MISSIONARY: I think I understand what you're saying. Since it seems like drinking tea would be medically good for you, not to drink it seems like a bad idea. Is that right?

INVESTIGATOR: Yes.

MISSIONARY: Let me show you something. In Doctrine and Covenants 89:9, we are told to not use "hot drinks."

INVESTIGATOR: So we can't even have soup or hot chocolate?

MISSIONARY: Not quite. Later, the Prophet Joseph Smith explained that "hot drinks" meant tea and coffee.

INVESTIGATOR: No offense, but I don't know if I can believe that.

MISSIONARY: Well, let's look at it this way.

If Joseph Smith really was a prophet, then we should follow what he said, right?

INVESTIGATOR: Yeah.

MISSIONARY: So the question that we have to decide isn't really about drinking tea. It's whether or not Joseph Smith was a prophet. And if the Book of Mormon is true, then we know that Joseph Smith was a prophet.

INVESTIGATOR: I see what you mean.

MISSIONARY: So the question is: Is the Book of Mormon true? Because if it is, then Joseph Smith was a prophet, and the revelation not to drink tea is from God.

INVESTIGATOR: So I need to find out whether the Book of Mormon is true.

MISSIONARY: Exactly.

* * *

As the missionary said, "The question is: Is the Book of Mormon true?"

I know that the Book of Mormon *is* the word

of God. Elder David A. Bednar said, "Intellectually I know the Book of Mormon is true; and I know it through personal experience as an author. And that type of knowledge is nice. But what is most important is the witness of the Spirit."[2]

I hope the intellectual evidences you've read about here strengthen your belief in the Book of Mormon. But as I said earlier, these intellectual evidences are not a substitute for seriously studying the Book of Mormon and praying with real intent to know if it is true (remember Moroni 10:4–5).

Have you read from the Book of Mormon and prayed about it? If not, I invite you to do so. If you have, please continue to drink deeply from its pages. The knowledge that comes as you do so will become the foundation of your testimony of Jesus Christ and His restored Church on the earth.

Notes

Introduction

Farrer, "The Christian Apologist," in Gibb, *Light on C. S. Lewis*, 26.

1. Condie, *Russell M. Nelson*, 118.

2. Benson, "The Keystone of Our Religion," *Ensign*, January 1992, 5.

Chapter 1: What's Up with Wordprints?

1. Hilton, "On Verifying Wordprint Studies," 101.

Chapter 2: What Would You Do If You Felt a Friend Betrayed You?

1. Anderson, *Investigating the Book of Mormon Witnesses*, 60.

2. Anderson, *Investigating the Book of Mormon Witnesses*, 76.

3. Anderson, *Investigating the Book of Mormon Witnesses*, 88.

4. Reynolds, *Book of Mormon Authorship Revisited*, 48.

5. Anderson, *Investigating the Book of Mormon Witnesses*, 129.

Chapter 3: How Fast Can You Write a Research Paper?

1. Backman, *Eyewitness Accounts of the Restoration*, 127.

2. Backman, *Eyewitness Accounts of the Restoration*, 127.

3. Bednar, *Come unto Christ,* Religious Lecture Series, 29
   January 2000.

Chapter 6: "Gotcha Now"—or So They Thought
1. Grant, Conference Report, April 1929, 129.

Chapter 7: Seven More Sticks
1. See Tvedtnes, *Book of Mormon and Other Hidden Books,*
   155.
2. Holland, *Students Need Teachers to Guide Them,* 2.

Conclusion
1. Benson, "The Book of Mormon Is the Word of God,"
   Ensign, January 1988, 4.
2. Bednar, *Come unto Christ,* Religious Lecture Series, 29
   January 2000.

Sources

Anderson, Richard Lloyd. *Book of Mormon Witnesses.* Available at maxwellinstitute.byu.edu

——. *Investigating the Book of Mormon Witnesses.* Salt Lake City: Deseret Book Company, 1981.

Backman, Milton V., Jr. *Eyewitness Accounts of the Restoration.* Salt Lake City: Deseret Book Company, 1986.

Bednar, David A. *Come unto Christ.* Religious Lecture Series. Ricks College, Rexburg, Idaho, 29 January 2000. Available at byui.edu/presentations

Bennett, Robert R. *Barley and Wheat in the Book of Mormon.* Available at maxwellinstitute.byu.edu

——. *Cement in the Book of Mormon.* Available at maxwellinstitute.byu.edu

Benson, Ezra Taft. "The Book of Mormon Is the Word of God." *Ensign,* January 1988, 3–5.

——. "The Keystone of Our Religion." *Ensign,* January 1992, 2–7.

Condie, Spencer J. *Russell M. Nelson: Father, Surgeon, Apostle.* Salt Lake City: Deseret Book, 2003.

Edwards, Boyd F., and W. Farrell Edwards. "Does Chiasmus Appear in the Book of Mormon by Chance?" *BYU Studies* 43, no. 2 (2004): 103–30. Available at byu studies.byu.edu

Farrer, Austin. "The Christian Apologist." In *Light on C. S. Lewis.* Comp. Jocelyn Gibb. New York: Harcourt and Brace, 1965.

fairwiki.org/index.php/Book_of_Mormon_anachronisms: Animals

fairwiki.org/index.php/FAIRwiki:Table_of_contents#Anac hronisms.3F

fairwiki.org/index.php/Olive_culture_in_the_Book_of_Mor mon

For the Strength of Youth. Salt Lake City: The Church of Jesus Christ of Latter-day Saints, 2001.

Grant, Heber J. Conference Report, April 1929, 128–31.

Hilton, John L. "On Verifying Wordprint Studies: Book of Mormon Authorship." *BYU Studies* 30, no. 3 (1990): 89–108. Available at byustudies.byu.edu

Holland, Jeffrey R. *Students Need Teachers to Guide Them.* CES Satellite Broadcast, 20 June 1992.

jefflindsay.com/BMEvidences.shtml

lightplanet.com/response/bofm.htm

Maxwell, Neal A. *Discipleship and Scholarship.* Address delivered at Brigham Young University, Provo, Utah, 27 September 1991. Available in *BYU Studies* 32, no. 3

(1992): 59, or at unicomm.byu.edu/president/documents/maxwell.htm

Peterson, Daniel C. *Evidences of the Book of Mormon.* Available at maxwellinstitute.byu.edu

Reynolds, Noel B. *The Authorship of the Book of Mormon.* Available at speeches.byu.edu

———. *Book of Mormon Authorship Revisited: Evidence for Ancient Origins.* Provo, Utah: FARMS [Foundation for Ancient Research and Mormon Studies], 1997.

Schaalje, G. Bruce, John L. Hilton, and John B. Archer. "Comparative Power of Three Author-Attribution Techniques for Differentiating Authors." *Journal of Book of Mormon Studies* 6, no. 1 (1997): 47–65. Available at maxwellinstitute.byu.edu

Sperry, Sidney B. *The Book of Mormon as Translation English.* Available at farms.byu.edu

Smith, Joseph. *Teachings of the Prophet Joseph Smith.* Sel. Joseph Fielding Smith. Salt Lake City: Deseret Book, 1976.

Tvedtnes, John A. *The Book of Mormon and Other Hidden Books: Out of Darkness unto Light.* Provo, Utah: FARMS [Foundation for Ancient Research and Mormon Studies], 2000.

———. "Hebraisms in the Book of Mormon: A Preliminary Survey." *BYU Studies* 11, no. 1 (1970): 50. Available at byustudies.byu.edu

Welch, John W. "Chiasmus in the Book of Mormon." *New Era,* February 1972, 6–11. Available at lds.org

——. "How Long Did It Take Joseph Smith to Translate the Book of Mormon?" *Ensign,* January 1988, 46.

——. "How Much Was Known about Chiasmus in 1829 When the Book of Mormon Was Translated?" Available at maxwellinstitute.byu.edu

——. "What Does Chiasmus in the Book of Mormon Prove?" In Noel B. Reynolds, *Book of Mormon Authorship Revisited.* Provo, Utah: FARMS [Foundation for Ancient Research and Mormon Studies], 1997.

Index